D0460981

The Moon Is La Luna

Silly Rhymes in English & Spanish

Rhymes by Jay M. Harris

Pictures by Matthew Cordell

Houghton Mifflin Company
Boston 2007

To my wife, Trudy, who is
my inspiration and my greatest supporter. —J.H.

A mi esposa hermosa, Julie. —M.C.

Text copyright © 2007 by Jay M. Harris
Illustrations copyright © 2007 by Matthew Cordell

www.houghtonmifflinbooks.com

The text of this book is set in 16-point TriplexLight.
The illustrations are pen and ink with watercolor.

Library of Congress Cataloging-in-Publication Data
Harris, Jay M.
The moon is la luna : silly rhymes in English & Spanish /
by Jay M. Harris ; illustrated by Matthew Cordell.
p. cm.
Summary: Easy-to-read text introduces Spanish words and rhymes
them with English ones that are sometimes very different, as well as
providing advice on using words that are much the same.
ISBN-13: 978-0-618-64645-6 (hardcover)
ISBN-10: 0-618-64645-0 (hardcover)
[1. Spanish language—Fiction. 2. Language and languages—Fiction. 3.
Humorous stories. 4. Stories in rhyme.] I. Cordell, Matthew, ill. II. Title.
PZ8.3.H24258Moo 2007
[E]—dc22
2006026082

Printed in Singapore
TWP 10 9 8 7 6 5 4 3 2 1

The moon is *la luna*.
The sun is *el sol*.
To say "Spanish" in Spanish,
You say *"Español."*

A river is *un río*.
When the river's cold, it's *frío*.
As the water turns chill,
It gets harder until
You can walk on *un río frío*.

A flower is called *una flor,*
Just like the floor you stand on.
If you pass out from its smell,
It's like the floor you land on!

The sea is *el mar*.
To float is *flotar*.
If you miss the boat,
You won't get too far
If you try to float
'Cross the sea in your car.

Un árbol is a tree.
Una roca is a rock.
I'd rather have *una roca*
Than *un árbol* in my sock.

Flaco means skinny.
Gordo means fat.
Flaco's my dog.
Gordo's my cat.

Don't drive in your *auto*
With your *gato* and *pato,*
'Cause a cat and a duck
In your car is bad luck!
If they must tag along,
Make them ride in your truck.

Grande is big.

Pequeño is small.

And *nada* is nothing at all.

A tail is *una cola,*
And it would NOT be nice
To request a frosty cola
And be told "Go sit on ice."

Soy beans, soy beans,
Eat them with beef or ham.
But *soy,* in Spanish, isn't beans.
Instead it means "I am!"

"Oh, no! It's *un mono*!" my grandmother said.
"Only a monkey would jump on the bed.
Act like a boy—be *un niño* instead."

Pies, in Spanish, are not pies,
Or anything else good to eat.
"Pee-ace," it's said,
So don't be misled—
Pies, in Spanish, are feet!

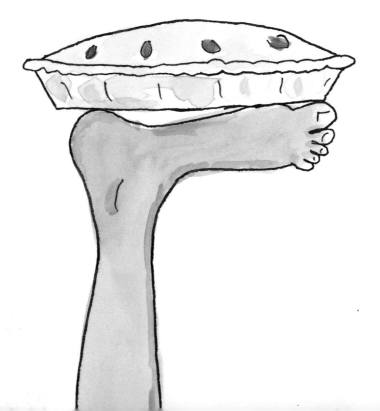

A tooth is *un diente*.
A tooth in the front is *en frente*.
My sister Kate
Is almost eight
And has no *diente en frente*.
It's the truth—
Not one tooth!

El pelo is hair.
("Peh-low" is what it is called.)
You may think that your hair
Is, at times, hard to bear,
But remember, without it you're bald.

Rápido is fast.
Despacio is slow.
Our ride is here,
It's time to go,
So don't be so
Despacio!

Yes is *sí*.
Like you swim in the sea.
More is *mas*.
Like moss on a tree.
So it's *Sí, mas por favor*—
Yes, please more.
Or, *No mas, por favor*—
Please, no more.

If you're eating meatballs and pasta,
When you've had enough, say *"Basta."*

To say "salt" in Spanish, just leave off the "t."
Some *sal* on my popcorn sounds yummy to me.
But hold *el pimiento,* and don't shake it, please,
Because pepper on popcorn can make people sneeze.
AAAHHCHOOO.

The word for "here" is *aquí*.
(It's said just like "a key.")
To unlock a lock,
Be first on your block
To hide a key *aquí*!
(In your sock?)

A light is called *una luz*.
(*Luz* is said like "loose.")
If *la luz* is loose,
You may say with a smirk
"Unless it is tighter,
La luz will not work!"

There's *un ratón en mi casa,*
But please don't fret,
That mouse in my house
Is my brother's pet.

When you take a nap, it's *una siesta*.
When you throw a party, it's *una fiesta*.
It would be best
To get a short rest,
So before *la fiesta, siesta!*

A bath is *un baño*.
A year is *un año*.
It is not enough, I fear,
To take one bath each year.

Una cama is a bed.
("Comma" is how it is said.)
A comma is placed in a sentence
To give the reader a rest.
Mi cama is placed in my bedroom.
I rest in that *cama* the best.

In *Español, papá* means "dad."
("paPA" is how it is said.)
But *papa* (said "POP-a") doesn't mean "dad,"
It means "potato" instead.
So watch how you say it,
Unless you would like
A potato to tuck you in bed.

Un oso is a bear,
And bears are big and hairy.
At night you'd best beware,
'Cause they are *oh so* scary!

In *Español,* a wolf is *un lobo*.
When it howls at the moon
It's a similar tune
To my sister playing her oboe.

A chair is *una silla*.
("See ya" is how it is said.)
So when your friends call "See ya!"
Yell "Chair!" to them instead.

Spanish Pronunciation Guide

a	ah.	As in *car*, *casa*.
e	eh.	As in *egg*, *Español*.
i	ee.	As in *feet*, *mi*.
o	oh.	As in *ocean*, *oso*.
u	oo.	As in *moon*, *luna*.
ll	y.	As in *year*, *silla*.
ñ	ny.	As in *canyon*, *niño*.
j	h.	As in *hair*, *José*.

Glossary

adiós goodbye

amigo, a friend

año year

aquí here

árbol tree

auto car

baño bath

basta enough

cama bed

casa house

cola tail

despacio slow

diente tooth

el the

en in

Español Spanish

fiesta party

flor flower

flaco skinny

flotar to float

frente front

frío cold

gato cat

gordo fat

grande big

hola hello

la the

lobo wolf

luna moon

luz light

mar sea

mas more

mi my

mono monkey

niña girl

niño boy

nada nothing

no no

oso bear

papá dad

papa potato

pato duck

pelo hair

perro dog

pequeño small

por favor please

pies feet

pimiento pepper

rápido fast

ratón mouse

río river

roca rock

sal salt

sí yes

siesta nap

silla chair

sol sun

soy I am

(Instead of saying, *"Yo soy,"* meaning literally "I am," in Spanish the *"yo"* or "I" can be dropped without affecting the meaning of the phrase.)

un, una a or an

yo I